AGELESS INDIA - 6

AGELESS INDIA - 6

ETHEREAL IMAGES

Sketches by
Mala Marwah

Series Editor
MALVIKA SINGH

LIMITED
EDITIONS

AN IMPRINT OF
ACADEMIC FOUNDATION

INTRODUCTION TO THE SERIES

This series of Notebooks was conceived as a vibrant and energetic representation of India, manifesting images of her past and present, her remarkable and infinite civilisation with its endless layers of diversity merging and melding into one another, creating a fabric of seamless transitions laced with overlaps of buoyant contradictions that are often unpredictable and mysterious, allowing for flights of the imagination, and leaving 'room for wonder'.

Through the pages of *Ageless India*, this extraordinary and finely nuanced, ever-evolving and contemporary destination on earth, continues to draw into its complex unstitched folds, the many stories and experiences, the influences and ideas that emerge from a 'planet', continually revolving ecliptically on its firm axis, sharing experience and endorsing a sublime unity in exciting and invigorating diversity.

The voyeur in us can use these books to exchange notes, share ideas, articulate intangible reflections in words, and more, to leave them as 'memories' that can be savoured today, as well as in the years to come, by family and friends, to keep the connect of the past with the future alive.

Ageless India will showcase the personalised 'India' of men and women impassioned by her many 'plots' and 'sub-plots', using the skill of their hands and eyes to capture for posterity, her changing avatars, her multiple expressions. The series will be infinite...

Malvika Singh
New Delhi 2015

AGELESS INDIA - 6

ETHEREAL IMAGES

About the Book note by the series editor

Series Editor
MALVIKA SINGH

Artist's Note

These drawings were made when I was a student forty years ago at the Faculty of Fine Arts, Baroda. The Maharaja Sayajirao University of Baroda supported a programme where students of the Faculty visited a site of artistic and historical importance on a study tour, and it was an eagerly anticipated event in the calendar.

The travelled in a large group, students and teachers, those who had opted for it, along with a maharaj to cook for us! Plastic water bottles, eat materials, the lot. Often we spread out on the floor of the platform or a terrace, spread with newspapers, and enjoyed our puris and vegetables after a day spent walking, studying and sketching.

To see the sulphites and paintings in the original spaces meant for them gave the ant an enhanced meaning and we imagined pilgrims and priests, children and vendors crowding these sites much as they did today, only further in time.

In the evenings we shared the day's sketchbooks, had our meal, sang or meant for a walk or visited the occasional market—if there was one. The even held the antakshari!

The two places we visited in my time were the Sun Temple at Konarak, Odisha, and the Ajanta caves and Ellora Temple in Maharastra. In this, our classroom without walls, we were stunned by the beauty we saw, humbled by the magical quality of the painter's and carver's art. Speaking for myself, I would not have exchanged this experience for anything in the world.

M.M.

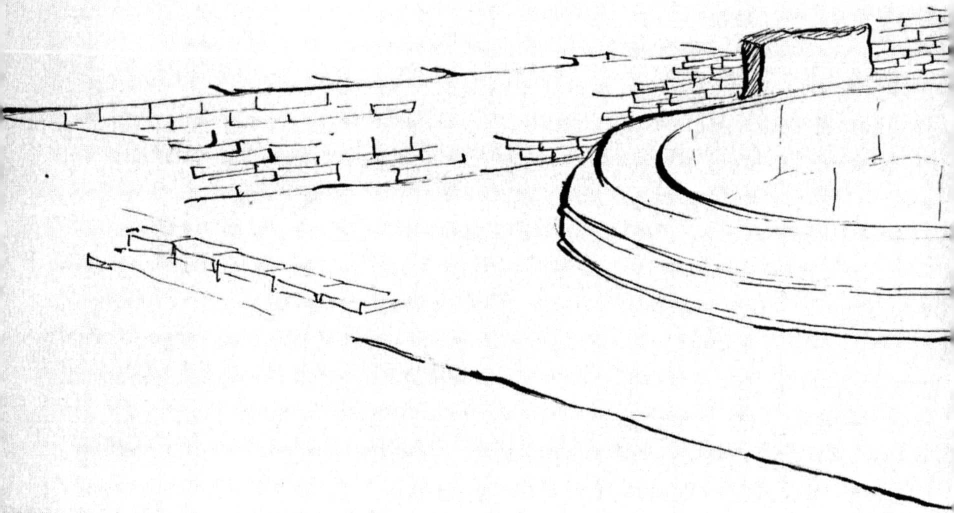

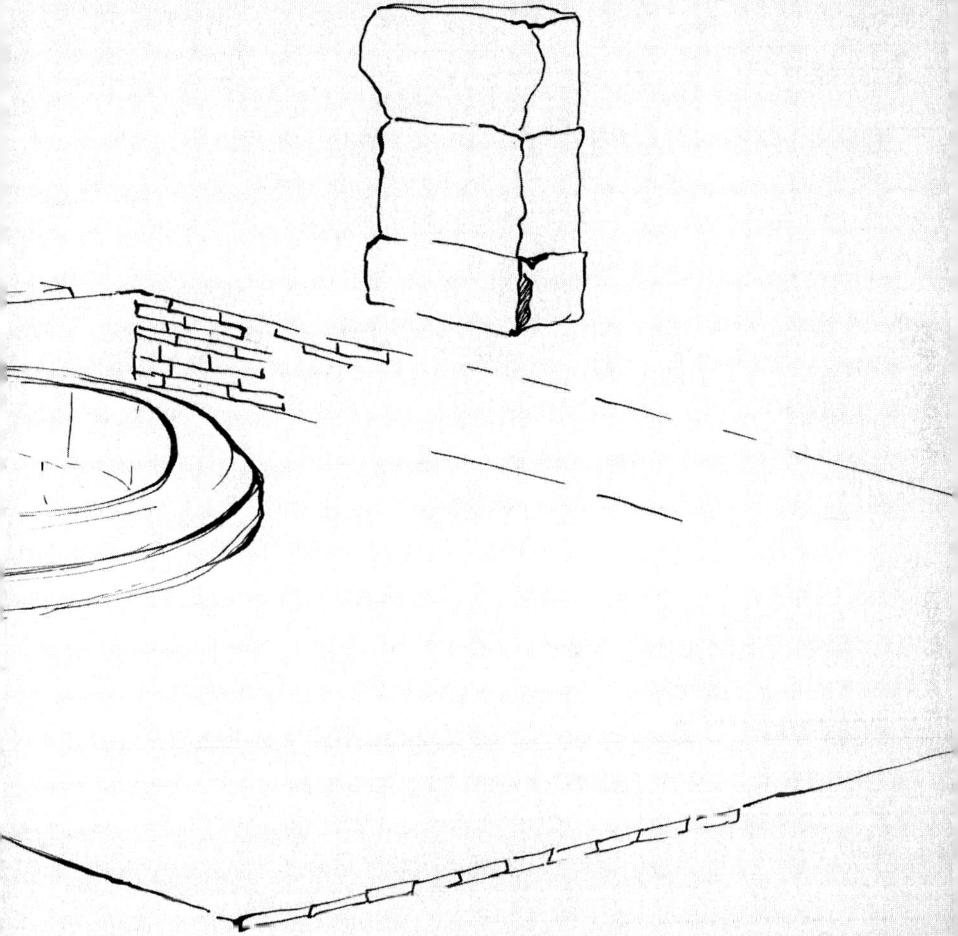

Rived well and terrace, Konarak Compound of Sun Temple, Odisha, 13th century.

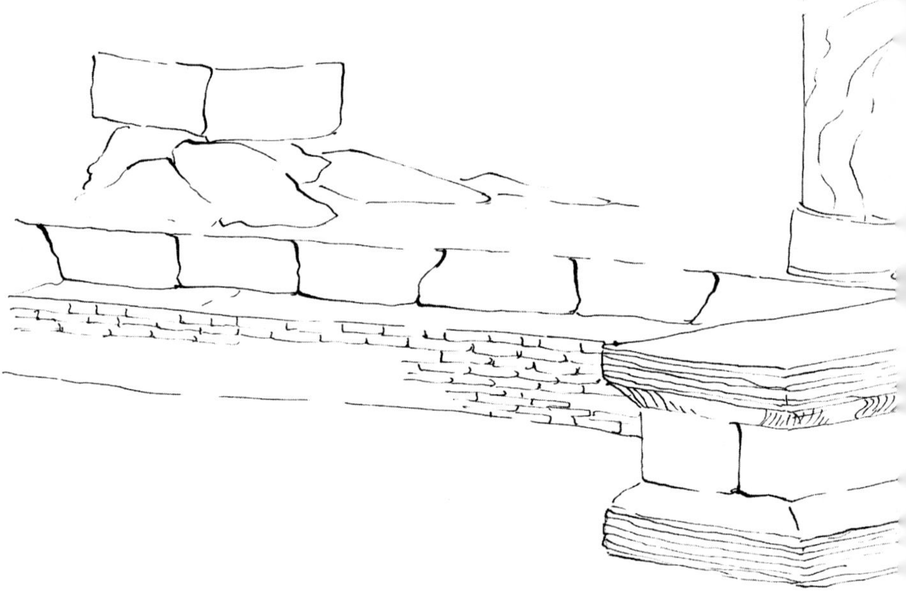

Pillars and terrace, Sun Temple.

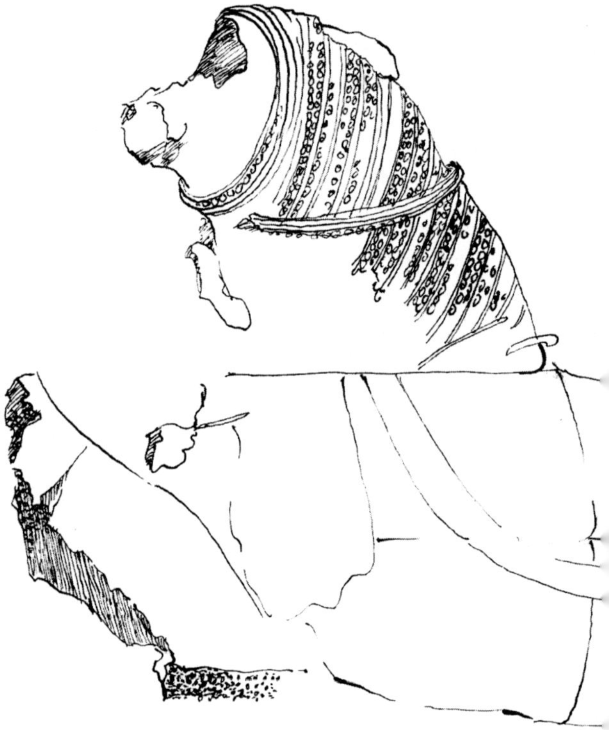

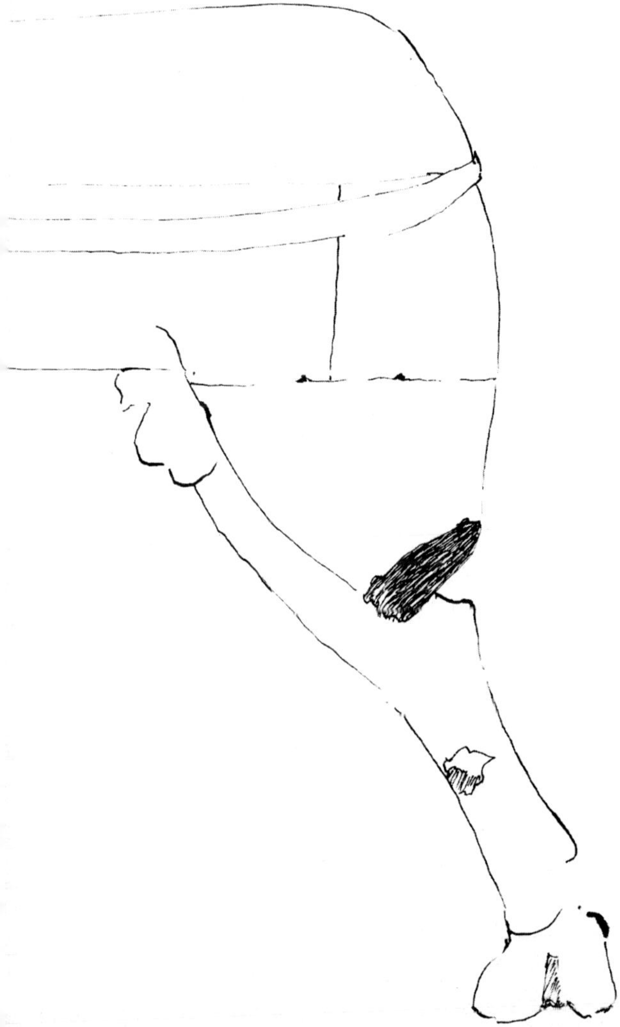

Body of life-size horse, Sun-Temple,
Head broken.

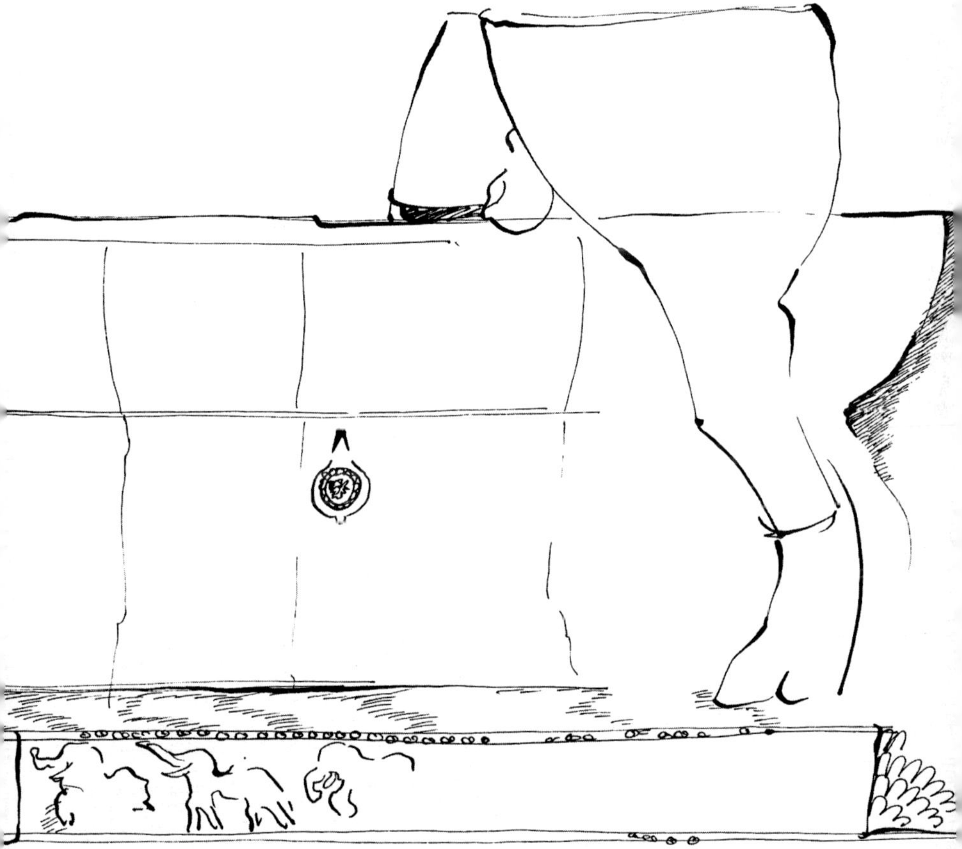

Life-size horse with frieze of animal beneath. Sun Temple.

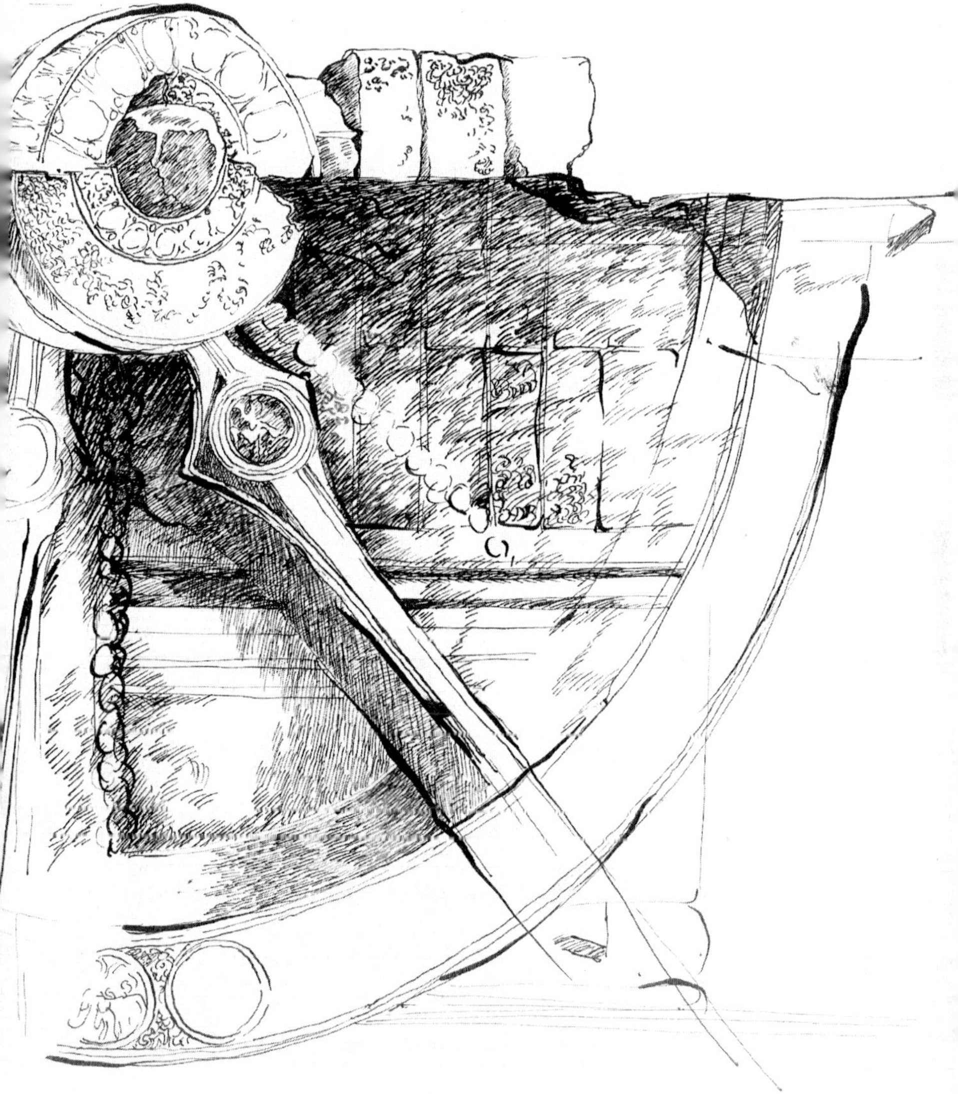

Gigantic Stone Wheel (12ft. diameter) One of six on platform, Sun Temple.

Steps to Nāta Mandir, showing lion as symbol of King Narasimhadeva I (1238-64).

Steps to Nāta Mandir.

Kanyās, female figures from Lingaraja Temple, Bhubaneswara; c.1100.

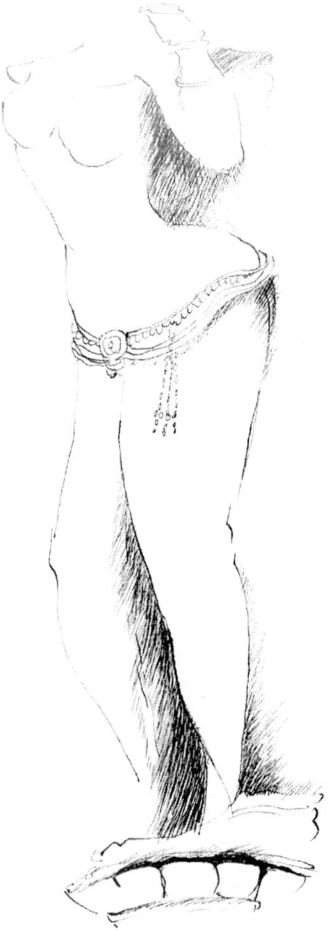

Kanyās, female figures from the beautiful Rajarani Temple, Odish, 11-12th century.
One holds up the branch of a tree, one extracts a thoru from her foot.

One of celestial stone musicians an upper story of jagmohana, Sun Temple.

Stone musician with stringed instrument, Sun Temple (museum).

Magnificent stone musician, Sun Temple (museum).

Kavya dressing her hair. Sun Temple.

'egetal scroll motives of an earlier
radition typical of Odishan archi-
ecture. Decoration with pearls,
ells, lotuses, leaves and waves
re seen.

Gava, or dwarf?, keepers of the riches under the earth, attendants of Ganesh, and servers to the dwarapalikas, kanyasa, and donors to the temple; Odishan feature. He attempts a tribhangi pose typical to Odishi dance.

This lovely stone elephant was sitting quite at peace with himself at the museum. I found the back view most pleasing. Instead of pen ink I used a soft crayon to suggest his small plump volume.

Horse with attendant, life-size stone. These suggest the equine beauty of the animals used to pull the Sun-God's chariot, which the Temple is designed to resemble.

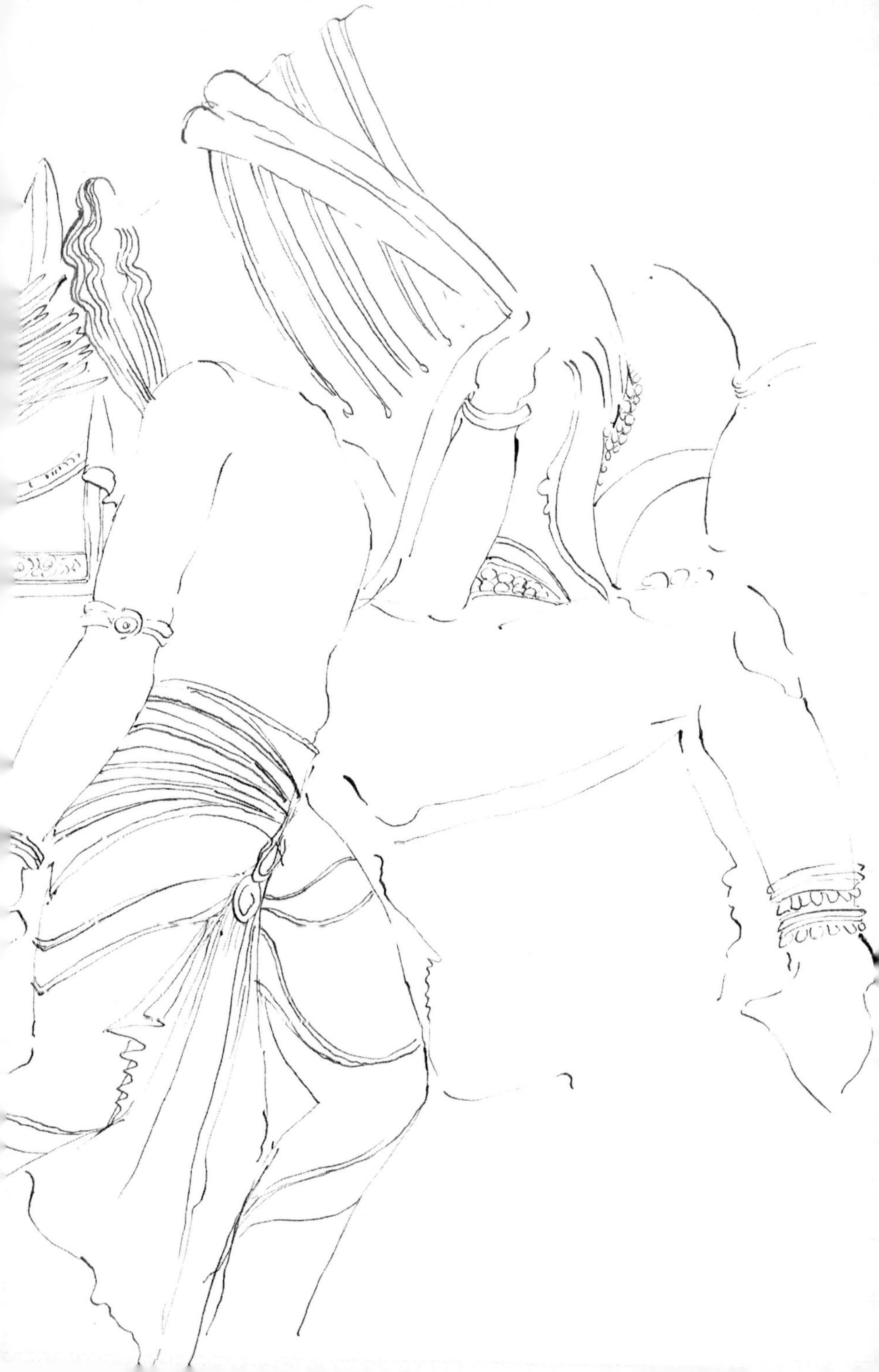

Life-size stone horse with attendant. The saddle, horses, trappings and the attendant is lower garment are delicately carved. Sun Temple.

Vovine figure showing details of diaphanous dress in the carving. Sun Temple.

Symbolic figure of Lion (after King Narasimhadeva) triumphing over evening as trampled elephant. Enhance to Nata Mandir. Sun Temple.

Colleague friend, Usha Nehru Patel. Like all good Kashmiris, found of fruit and nuts. Student of Painting.

ha + oranges

n in RATjLY TRAIN which is as is.

Nandan Kudhyadi, filmmaker, started his career as Fine Arts student at Baroda. Observer of detail and composition, admirer of Guru Dutt , Akbar Padamsee and much else. He once struck a pose, one foot carefully placed before the other, while sipping cough syrup from the cap of the bottle because it had a drop of alcohol in it deserved to be savoured...

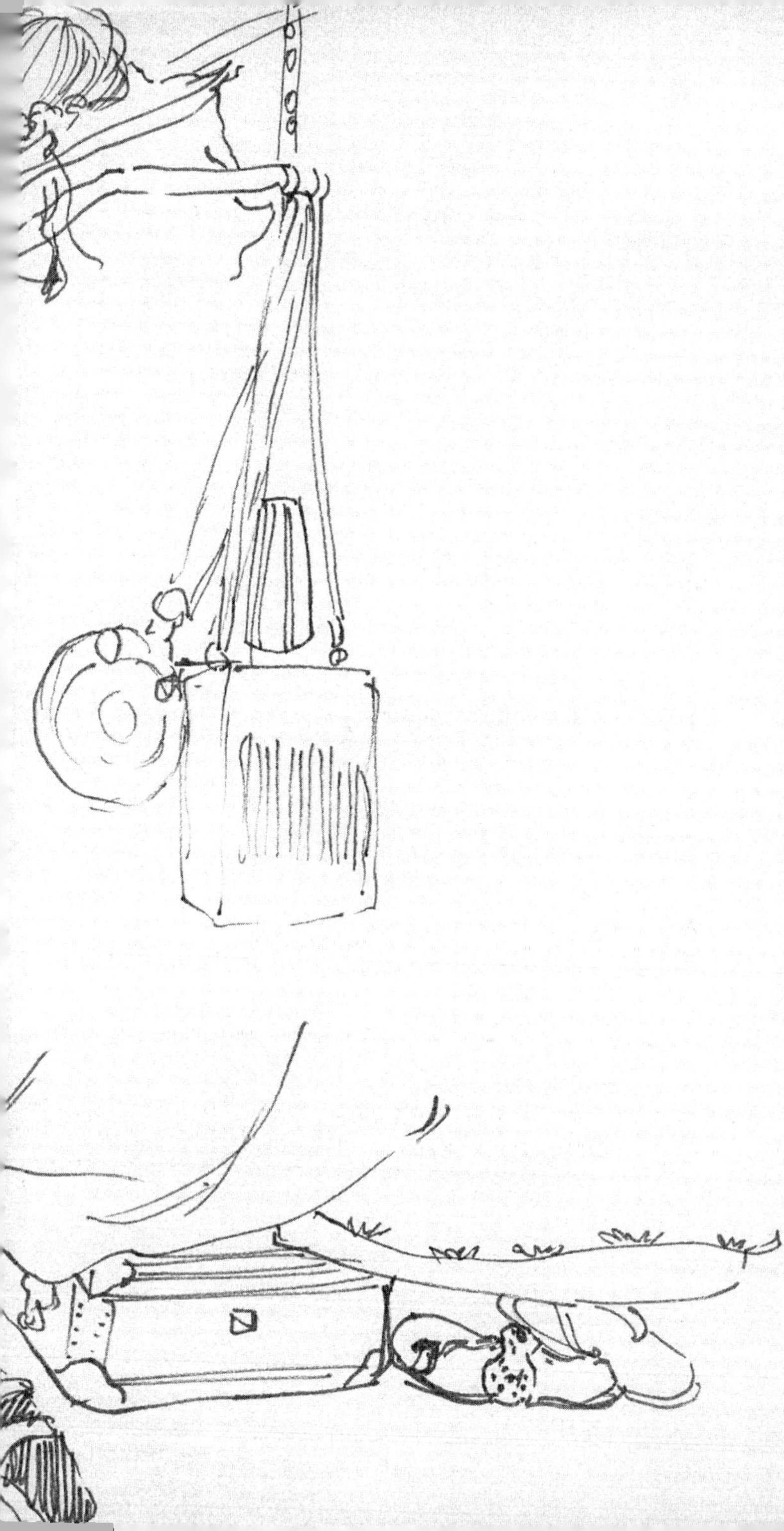

This was how we travelled. The two berths above and below were joined by sturdy wooden planks fitted with iron clamps. Sometimes we sketched each other, told tall tales, imitated our teachers or kicked up a din. Life as a Fine-Artic can be fun.

Lingaraja Temple
Bhubaneswara April.

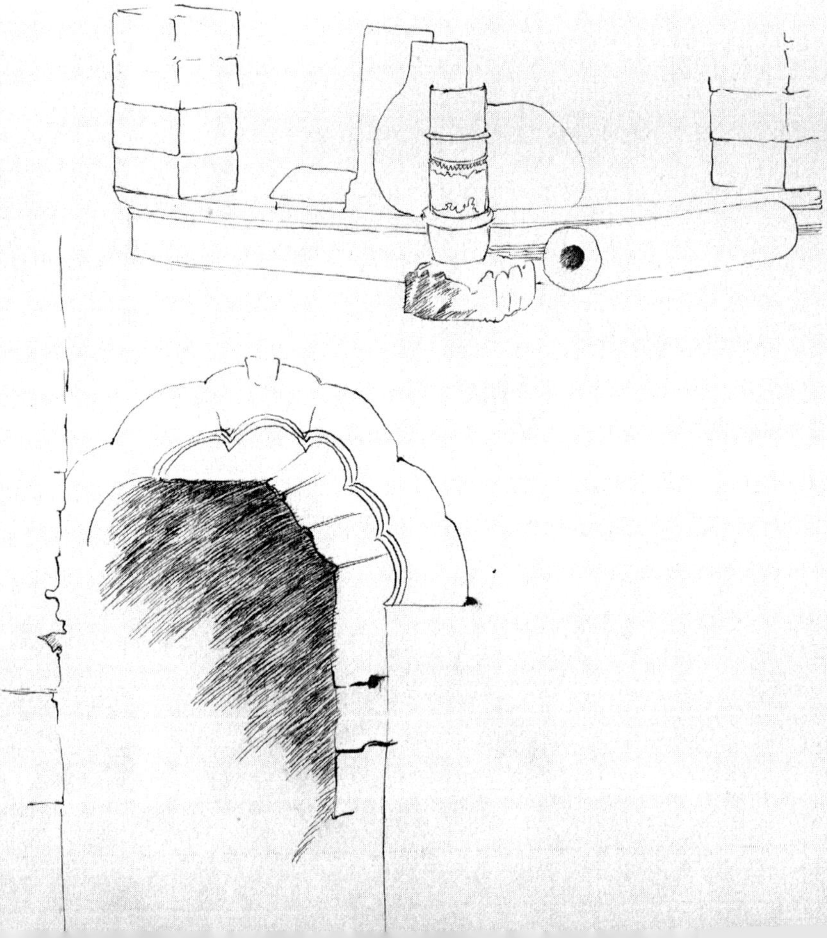

Lingaraja Temple, Bhubaneswara. Lovingly garlanded Nandi bull with fresh flowers; terrace with pieces of broken masonry; beautifully carved doorway.

Lingaraj Temple
Bhubaneswar
Ap— '75

Lingaraja Temple. Decorative animal detail of elephant, lion in two different carvings.

Lingaraja Temple. Elephant nesting, with lonely pillar lying quite forgotten next to time.

Lingaraja Temple. South-west gate,
Bhubneswara.

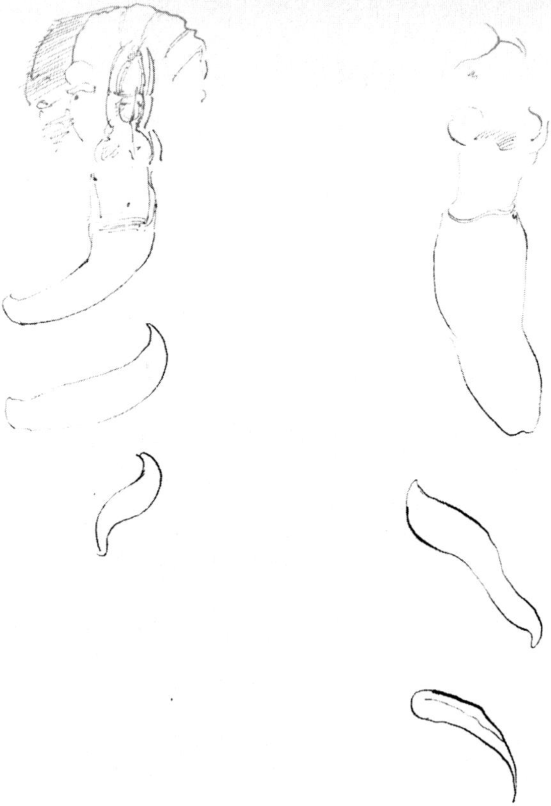

Details of the beautiful Rajarani Temple, 11th c. Containing details characteristic of the original Odisha invention, the large round naga/nagini pilaster, the serpent's tail curling around it in a wide spiral. Also seen at the Mukteshwara Temple.

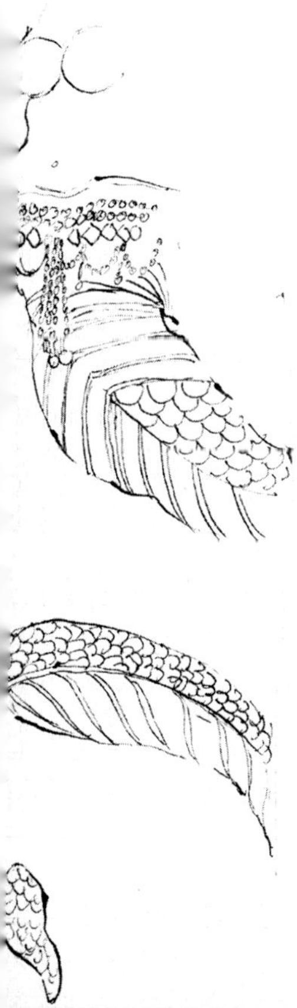

Portal of the Rajarani Temple, with victoriously grimacing simha figure atop.

Lingaraja Temple. Portion of wall, South-west

Lingaraja Mandir
Shiva Shrine
Bhubaneswar

Lingaraja Temple. Shiva shrine, Bhubaneswara, 1100 circa.

Mukteshwara Temple. This beautiful temple is the only Odishan temple with a torana gateway like this one, and its proportions and designated sections are in perfect harmony. It is small perfect temple. c. 950-75.

Parashurameswara Temple compound, Bhubaneswara. c. 650-80. Occupants of thatched place, smoking, watching the world go by. Part of masonry and tree.

Bindu Sagara, the ghat next a large pool. Bhubaneswara mother is trying to get her little boy's face (sp. his nose)

Some miles away, in the opposite direction from Bhubaneswara, twenty or more monastic dwellings have been carved out of the sloping sides of two hills, Khandagiri and Udaygiri, which face each other. One inscription informs us that King Kharavela (1st century B.C.) a devout Jain, had these caves and cells made for the use of monks. Vegetal and fruiting and motifs decorate the tops of the arcades. Otherwise the spaces are simple.

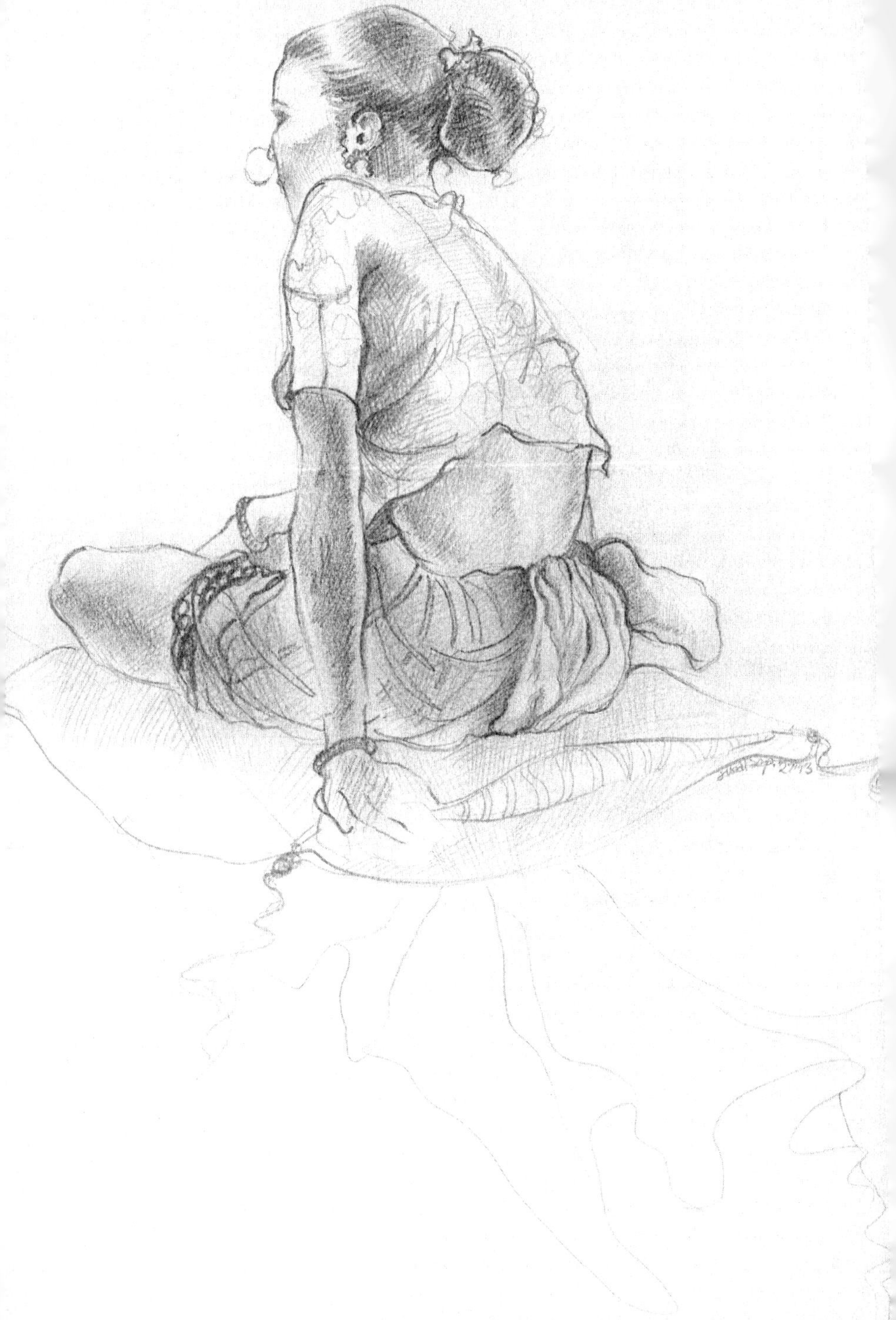

Pencil drawing of one of our models in the Painting department. They were mostly tribal woman, some with striking facial features.

Deities and pensevages? in Ajanta, very likely part a jataka. Cave unknown. Ink and wash.

Chaitya-type enhance to one of the caves at Ajanta; clump of bomboo growing wild bearby.

Yasin mia, young son of Abbujan, who run a tea-shop outside the Dak Bungalow at Khuldabad where we stayed. This was our favourite place for 'adda' tea and chatting in between working and studying hours.

ear the Dak Bungalow smaller
ut study, old outhouses that very
kely accommodated stores?, clerks
nd files. The trees clearly? were
ncient

I decided to record the relaxing and dozing arrangements on the verandah. To the right was a large-ish rook which, we were told by the female attendants at the Dak Bungalow was occupied by Meena Kumari when they had filmed for Pakeezah at nearby Khuldabad. Said she used a fragrant soap for her bath, and scarcely ever spoke a word. It seemed rude to ask any questions.

View from the tea-shop. These were all ruins/monuments in need of repair and conservation. The domes with the frill of petal like decoration at the lower rim is typical of domes of this period. Those spaces mere occupied, as the line of laundry suggests.

Tea-shop in Khuldabad with posters advertising Berkeley Cigarettes and Pakeezah.

Next to Shama-Yaadgaar Tea House,
Khuldabad.

Daulatabad Fort. Said to be one of the most powerful forts of the Deccan with multiple moats and walls, excellent canon and defenses which however failed to prevent it being captured and occupied by a series of rulers. To the right of this massive canon is seen the slender minaret of the Char? Minar.

Daulatabad Fort. Maharashtrian man in typical headgear prepares a chillum. It's three in the afternoon, best to sketch the fort and its environs from outside so we can get back to the Rest House soon. Climbing forts is tiring work.

Husain Ali + biri shop

Husain Ali was selling some fruit so I had some; I wasn't interested in the biris.

TODAY'S SPECIAL
SANDWITCH
BREAD BUTTER
PATIES, SAMOSA
KACHORI-KOBI VADA
RAVA MASALA DOSA
RAVA SADA DOSA
RAVA MASALA SADA
DAHI VADA
DAHI MISAL

Kamakshi Bhawan, aurangabad.
Blue and white plastic curtains.
Clean. We replenished ourselves.

Bela in x morning.

Holly K
Study tour
Ajanta/Ellora Dec.'73.
Parul

Early morning in the girl's room.

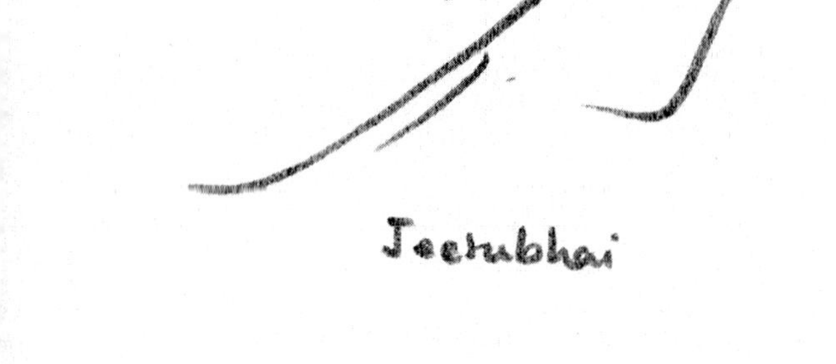

Jeetubhai

Jeetubhai.

Small alcoves, sculptural decoration in recesses at Ajanta.

Buddha with hand raised in bless-
ing. Ink, pen replaced with brush.
Looks like a chaitya hall. Ajanta.

Chauri-bearer, ajanta. Auspicious figure.

Pillars in a chaitya-hall, lotiform and other decoration on capitals.

Entrance to one of the caves, Ajanta. A shade has been erected to protect the painting on the walls of the shallow verandah.

Rock-hewn steps at Ajanta.

Ellona
Dec-25'73

ery likely Shiva. Powerful figure
espite crumbling condition. This
s outside Ellora, as you enter the
omplex.

The famous figure of Ravana shaking mount Kailash. Imprisoned in the bonds of Shiva's abode, Lankesh stretches his arms to uproot the mountain but is stilled by Shiva's toe. This amazing sculpture is carved almost entirely in the round, a dark recess behind.

Donor figure, Ellora, with beautifully carved pillar behind.

Donor figure, Ellora, with beautifully carved pillar before.

Varahavatar, Ellora.

Dwarapalika of Amazonian proportions, with ornamented girdle and neck and arm ornaments, Ellora. In some places the dwarapalika is attended by a gaña (dwarf), also suitably attired in ornaments.

Dwarapalika. Considered auspicious.

Dwarapalika.

Durga with Vahana.

Shiva in Tandav posture, Ellora.

Female figure suggesting fertility.
Prayed to for offspring.

Apsara, air-borne deity. Prayed to for boons.

First published in 2016
by
LIMITED EDITIONS
an imprint of

ACADEMIC FOUNDATION

Delhi Sales Office:
4772-73/23 Bharat Ram Road,
(23 Ansari Road), Darya Ganj,
New Delhi - 110 002 (India).
Tel : +91-11-23245001 / 02.
Fax : +91-11-23245005.

Corporate Office:
No. 35, Sector 7,
IMT Manesar,
Gurgaon - 122050.
Haryana (India).
Tel: +91-124-4215070 / 71.

E-mail : books@academicfoundation.com
www.academicfoundation.org

Ageless India, Book 6
Ethereal Images
Sketches by Mala Marwah

Series Editor: Malvika Singh

ISBN 13: 9789332702066

Designed, printed and bound by
The Book Mint, New Delhi.
www.thebookmint.in